**AMERICAN NURSES
ASSOCIATION**

D0711789

CORRECTIONS NURSING:
SCOPE AND STANDARDS
OF PRACTICE

nurses
books
.org

The Publishing Program of ANA

AMERICAN NURSES ASSOCIATION
SILVER SPRING, MARYLAND
2007

Library of Congress Cataloging-in-Publication data

Corrections nursing : scope and standards of practice /American Nurses Association.
    p. ; cm.
    Includes bibliographical references and index.
    ISBN-13: 978-1-55810-247-7 (pbk.)
    ISBN-10: 1-55810-247-7 (pbk.)
        1. Prison nurses—Standards.   2. Nursing—Standards.   3. Prisoners—Medical care—Standards.   I. Title.
        [DNLM: 1. Nursing—standards—Practice Guideline.   2. Prisons—Practice Guideline. WY 125 A516c 2007]

RT63.C6776 2007
    610.73—dc22   2007000675

The American Nurses Association (ANA) is a national professional association. This ANA publication— *Corrections Nursing: Scope and Standards of Practice*—reflects the thinking of the nursing profession on various issues and should be reviewed in conjunction with state board of nursing policies and practices. State law, rules, and regulations govern the practice of nursing, while *Corrections Nursing: Scope and Standards of Practice* guides nurses in the application of their professional skills and responsibilities.

Published by Nursesbooks.org
The Publishing Program of ANA

American Nurses Association
8515 Georgia Avenue, Suite 400
Silver Spring, MD 20910-3492
1-800-274-4ANA
http://www.nursesbooks.org/

ANA is the only full-service professional organization representing the nation's 2.7 million Registered Nurses through its 54 constituent member associations. ANA advances the nursing profession by fostering high standards of nursing practice, promoting the economic and general welfare of nurses in the workplace, projecting a positive and realistic view of nursing, and lobbying the Congress and regulatory agencies on healthcare issues affecting nurses and the public.

Design: Scott Bell, Arlington, VA; Freedom by Design, Alexandria, VA; Stacy Maquire, Sterling, VA ~ *Composition*: House of Equations, Inc., Arden, NC ~ *Editing*: Lisa Munsat Anthony, Chapel Hill, NC ~ *Proofreading & Indexing*: Steven A. Jent, Denton, TX ~ *Printing*: McArdle Printing, Upper Marlboro, MD

First printing January 2007.

ISBN-13: 978-1-55810-247-7   ISBN-10: 1-55810-247-7   SAN: 851-3481
07SSCN   2M   01/07

ACKNOWLEDGMENTS

Work Group Members

Kleanthe Caruso, MSN, RN, CCHP, CNAA, BC, Chairperson
Kathleen Bachmeier, MS, RN, BC
Patricia Blair, JD, LLM, MSN, RN
Arlene Chapman, RN, CCHP
Margaret M. Collatt, BSN, RN, CCHP-A
Catherine I. Fogel, PhD, RN,C, WHNCNP
Gail W. Fricks, BA, RN, CCHP
Rob Hofacre, BSN, MCRP, RN
JoRene Kerns, BSN, RN, CCHP
Jane McNeely, ARNP
Jacqueline Moore, PhD, RN, CCHP-A
Sue Moul, RN, CCHP-A
Mary Muse, MSN, RN, CCHP
M. Kay Northrup, BSN, RN, CCHP
Barbara Skeen, RN

ANA Staff

Carol J. Bickford, PhD, RN,BC—Content editor
Yvonne Daley Humes, MSA—Project coordinator
Matthew Seiler, RN, Esq.—Legal counsel

Winifred Carson-Smith, JD—Consultant

CONTENTS

PREFACE

In 2002 the American Nurses Association convened the volunteer work group of registered nurses tasked with the responsibility to review and revise the 1995 *Scope and Standards of Nursing Practice in Correctional Facilities*. The nurses held various positions in state and local adult and juvenile corrections and detention facilities, academic institutions, professional organizations, and healthcare facilities, and contributed a diverse perspective in all discussions.

The work group used *Code of Ethics for Nurses with Interpretive Statements* (2001); *Nursing's Social Policy Statement, 2nd Edition* (2003); and *Nursing: Scope and Standards of Practice* (2004) as foundational resources and completed its work via telephone conference calls and electronic mail communications. In 2004 a draft document was posted at ANA's web site (www.NursingWorld.org) for a 60-day public comment period. The work group reviewed each resultant comment and further revised the draft as necessary. In 2006 the Congress on Nursing Practice Committee on Nursing Practice Standards and Guidelines completed two reviews of the draft *Corrections Nursing: Scope and Standards of Practice* against established review criteria. Recommended revisions were completed before the ANA's Congress on Nursing Practice and Economics conducted a final review in fall 2006. The edits recommended by the Congress members to improve clarity have also been incorporated.

CORRECTIONS NURSING:
SCOPE OF PRACTICE

Corrections nursing is the practice of nursing and the delivery of patient care within the unique and distinct environment of the criminal justice system. The criminal justice system includes jails, prisons, juvenile detention centers, substance abuse treatment facilities, and other facilities.

Health Care in Correctional System Settings

Through most of its history, the United States corrections system had little or no health care available to inmates, as the courts typically took a detached approach to correctional issues and avoided interfering in the administration and operation of correctional facilities. This gave corrections administrators enormous freedom with little regulation or accountability imposed on daily operations. Public interest was minimal, and government agencies saw no reason to pour tax money into the prison system. The lack of oversight contributed to serious abuses behind the walls of correctional institutions.

The civil rights movement in the 1960s focused public attention on reform and improving conditions for the less fortunate. The inevitable scrutiny of conditions and practices in correctional facilities forced the American judicial system to begin to respond to inmate claims.

In 1976, the United States Supreme Court established a constitutional standard for inmate health care in the Texas case, *Estelle v. Gamble*. Inmate Gamble claimed that prison officials inflicted undue suffering on him when they failed to provide adequate care for an injury sustained in prison. The court ruled that "...deliberate indifference to serious medical needs of prisoners constitutes the 'unnecessary and wanton infliction of pain,' *Gregg v. Georgia, supra,* at 173 (joint opinion), proscribed by the Eighth Amendment. This is true whether the indifference is manifested by prison doctors in their response to the prisoner's needs or by prison guards in intentionally denying or delaying access to medical care or intentionally interfering with the treatment once prescribed. Regardless of how evidenced, deliberate indifference to a prisoner's serious illness or injury states a cause of action under § 1983" (*Estelle v. Gamble* 1976).

The decision led to several reforms in inmate litigation that included the following list of inmate rights related to health care:

- The right to access care
- The right to professional judgment
- The right to care that is ordered
- The right to informed consent
- The right to refuse treatment
- The right to medical confidentiality

Federal enforcement of these rights forced correctional agencies to restructure their inmate healthcare systems. During the years since *Estelle v. Gamble*, the development of both case law and national standards on correctional health care have affirmed that prisoners had a right to be free of "deliberate indifference to their serious healthcare needs."

Population Served

At the end of 2005, over 7 million people were on probation, in jail or prison, or on parole. This represents 3.2% of all U.S. adult residents or one out of every 32 adults. After dramatic increases in the 1980s and 1990s, the incarceration rate has leveled off at an average annual increase of 3.4 % (Bureau of Justice Statistics 2004). The June 2004 Juvenile Offenders and Victims National Report Series indicated that an estimated 134,011 youth were held in 2,939 facilities on October 27, 1999 (U.S. Department of Justice 2004). That total does not include juveniles under the age of 18 who are held in adult facilities.

Today's inmates are older and sicker and remain imprisoned longer when compared to the inmates of 20 years ago. In general, inmates come from socioeconomic groups at high risk for poor health and have not had access to regular healthcare services or proper treatment for medical conditions. They also have a disproportionately greater number of chronic illnesses and infectious diseases than the non-incarcerated population.

The incidence of HIV/AIDS in prisons and jails is substantially higher than in the population at large due to an over-representation of those with a history of high-risk behaviors. The CDC reports that in 1997 approximately 17% of all persons with the human immunodeficiency virus (HIV) had been released from corrections facilities (www.cdc.gov). As of 2001, state and federal prisoners known to be positive for HIV and confirmed AIDS cases totaled 24,147 (21,268 male and 2,265 female) (*Sourcebook of Criminal Justice Statistics* 2003).

Tuberculosis is one of the most threatening infectious diseases facing correctional systems. An estimated 35% of all persons with active TB cases in 1996 passed through the correctional system. In 2002 the National Commission on Correctional Health Care reported that the prevalence of active TB among inmates is between 4 and 17 times greater than among the total U.S. population (NCCHC 2002, p. *xi*). A study of U.S. surveillance data from 1993 to 2003 showed that 3.7% of all TB cases were reported within correctional systems. TB case rates for federal and state prisons were 29.4% and 24.3% per 100,000, respectively, compared to 6.7% per 100,000 in the general population. Inmates with TB also are more likely than the general population to forgo treatment (MacNeil 2005).

Hepatitis C, identified in 1989, has infected an estimated 3.9 million Americans. The most common form of transmission is through intravenous drug use. Approximately 83% of the nation's drug users are incarcerated at some time, and research indicates that 80% of inmates have a history of substance abuse (NCCHC 2002).

Advances in health care, longer prison terms, mandatory sentences, and more restrictive policies are keeping inmates in prison longer with lower chances of parole. This results in a much older resident population. "From 1992 to January 1, 2001, the number of state and federal inmates age 50 and older increased from 41,586 to 113,358, a staggering increase of 172.6%" (Anno et al. 2004, p. 7). In 2004 almost 240,000 inmates in our nation's prisons were age 45–54 and more than 16,000 were age 55 or older (American Correctional Association 2005a). In 2005, the average proportion of elderly inmates in state prison systems was 5.36% (American Correctional Association 2005b).

Inmates suffer from age-related conditions earlier in life. Personal histories of poor nutrition, lack of preventive care, and high-risk behavior such as smoking and drug use are all common in the general incarcerated population. This makes a 50-year-old inmate's health status comparable to that of a 65-year-old living in the community.

Women are the fastest growing segment of the correctional population. At year end 2003, the 101,179 women in prison comprised 6.9% of the state and federal prison population (Bureau of Justice Statistics 2004). Although more than half of these women are under the age of 35, the majority have unhealthy past lifestyles which include drug and alcohol abuse, sex work, and multiple partners, which put them at high risk for chronic and communicable diseases (Anno 1997).

In addition to basic healthcare needs, these women have special healthcare needs associated with their reproductive systems and thus pose a great challenge in the correctional healthcare system geared to house male inmates. Approximately 6% are pregnant on admission to jails and prisons and account for an estimated 8,820 of the 3.8 million births in the United States each year. Due to unhealthy lifestyles prior to incarceration, most of these pregnancies are classified as high risk (Greenfeld and Snell 1999). In a 2003 survey, pelvic exams, prenatal/postpartum services, mammograms, and pap smears were provided in all state systems surveyed, while reproductive counseling was offered in 77% of the reporting systems (American Correctional Association 2004).

Gender differences continue, with women having higher rates of diabetes, HIV, and sexually transmitted diseases, as well as higher rates of serious mental illnesses, drug abuse, depression, and other emotional problems in comparison with the male population. Consequently this results in women offenders using healthcare services more frequently than do their male counterparts (Goldkuhle 1999).

The deinstitutionalization of persons with mental illness over the last several decades has had a dramatic impact on the corrections environment. New therapies, decreased insurance reimbursements, and tightening state and local healthcare budgets have resulted in decreased length of stay and a drastic reduction in the number of state and county mental hospitals and inpatient beds. In 1970, there were approximately 368,000 beds in mental institutions. By 1992 that number had decreased to 84,000 beds. Lack of available community financial and social system supports has therefore resulted in persons with mental illness often becoming nomads who eventually end up residing in ever-increasing numbers in America's jails and prisons. Estimates indicate that 10–20% of inmate populations are suffering from major psychiatric disorders and require mental health services.

Nurses in the Corrections Environment

The history of corrections nursing began as early as 1797 with the opening of the New York City Newgate Prison. Its warden, Thomas Eddy, believed that criminals could be rehabilitated, and he established a school for the inmates as well as the first prison hospital and pharmacy. However, nursing as a professional presence in the correctional setting did not appear until the 1960s, and it began to gain visibility toward the end of the twentieth century.

Rena Murtha, a pioneer in corrections nursing, described entering a large correctional facility where the nurse was perceived as a "tool of the warden, a slave of the physician and an unknown to the patient" (1975). Since that time, corrections nursing practice has evolved into a variety of essential roles ranging from primary health care to management and administration. Today's corrections nurse is a respected member of the correctional system staff.

Just as it is difficult to ascertain the numbers and characteristics of the corrections population, this nursing specialty continues to be hidden in the statistical reporting about nurses and their employment and work settings. For example, the only reference to this nursing specialty in the 2000 National Sample Survey of Registered Nurses is the projected number of 18,033 registered nurses working in prisons or jails (USDHHS 2002). The *Sourcebook of Criminal Justice Statistics 2003* does not report the numbers of registered nurses or other healthcare providers working in correctional settings in its statistics and tables. Likewise, the American public is unaware of the complex conditions and great strains that face nurses working in correctional healthcare settings.

Correctional systems are under increasing pressure from the courts to provide adequate and humane levels of health care with limited resources and little public sympathy. Social and political conditions facing nurses in these settings are demanding and appeal to the noblest of humanitarian instincts. Nurses are often the foundation of the correctional healthcare system and in many cases the only providers of healthcare services in those systems. Correctional systems meet their responsibility to provide adequate and safe healthcare services to those incarcerated by using the expertise and unique knowledge and skills of registered nurses.

Nurses can often experience personal and professional conflict in these practice settings. In many cases, nurses are direct employees of the correctional facility and may be in the same organizational hierarchy as the correctional officers. On one hand, they are employees of an institution whose mission is security and public safety. On the other hand, they are healthcare providers whose mission is health and wellness. There is firm support in national standards to support the restriction of nurse participation in activities related strictly to security (NCCHC 2002). The focus on security may, at times, conflict with the provision of health services. For example, the goals of security may create a condition of conflict by considering healthcare access to be a privilege versus a right.

The registered nurse is an essential part of the correctional system and faces the daily challenges of providing health care in that setting. It is imperative that nurses in correctional settings recognize their professional responsibility for role development and clarification based on a commitment to quality nursing care according to recognized standards. The American Nurses Association and other organizations, such as the American Correctional Health Services Association, the American Correctional Association, and the Academy of Correctional Health Professionals, are membership organizations that serve as a forum for current issues and needs confronting corrections nurses. As the correctional system grows and continues to evolve, the corrections nurse will remain the advocate to ensure that patients are at an optimal state of physical and mental health to become productive citizens when they rejoin the community.

Principles of Corrections Nursing

Nursing is the protection, promotion, and optimization of health and abilities, prevention of illness and injury, alleviation of suffering through the diagnosis and treatment of human response, and advocacy in the care of individuals, families, communities, and populations (ANA 2004, p. 7). Nursing is a science and an art, the essence of which is caring for and respecting human beings, including those in the corrections environment. The following principles serve as the underpinning for corrections nursing:

- A registered nurse's primary duty in the corrections setting is to restore and maintain the health of patients in a spirit of compassion, concern, and professionalism.

- Each patient, regardless of circumstances, possesses intrinsic value and should be treated with dignity and respect.

- Each encounter with patients and families should portray professionalism, compassion, and concern.

- Each patient should receive quality care that is cost-effective and consistant with the latest treatment parameters and clinical guidelines.

- Patient confidentiality and privacy should be preserved.

- Nurses should collaborate with other healthcare team members, correctional staff, and community colleagues to meet the holistic needs of patients, which include physical, psychosocial, and spiritual aspects of care.

- Nurses should encourage each individual through patient and family education to take responsibility for disease prevention and health promotion.

- Each nurse maintains responsibility for monitoring and evaluating nursing practice necessary for continuous quality improvement.

- Nursing leadership should promote the highest quality of patient care through application of fair and equitable policies and procedures in collaboration with other healthcare services team members and corrections staff.

- Nursing services should be guided by nurse administrators who foster professional and personal development. These responsible leaders are sensitive to employee needs; give support, praise, and recognition; and encourage continuing education, participation in professional organizations, and generation of knowledge through research.

Role of the Corrections Nurse

Registered nurses working in corrections settings must demonstrate the essence of nursing in a practice setting and work environment that does not have health care as its primary mission. The care and judgment required to meet patients' needs rest with the nurse's assessment. Matters of nursing judgment are solely the domain of the registered nurse and may be challenged in such an environment without a supporting healthcare services infrastructure.

The incarcerated vary from youth to aged adults, include men and women, and are individuals of all racial and ethnic backgrounds who are often disenfranchised, economically challenged, educationally limited, and largely ignored by society. These people frequently enter the corrections system with communicable and chronic diseases and complications resulting from a previous lack of appropriate healthcare services. Corrections nurses work to limit the healthcare disparities experienced by this unique and extremely diversified corrections population.

Corrections nurses are expected to deliver care to all patients with compassion, empathy, commitment, competency, dedication, and a positive attitude. Although the length of incarceration differs in the various settings, corrections nurses play an integral role in providing healthcare services to this population through patient education, patient advocacy, and the delivery of patient care.

It is inappropriate for nurses to be involved in the security aspects of the facility and disciplinary decisions or committees. Corrections nurses must be vigilant in maintaining a healthcare role and not participate in nontherapeutic court-ordered procedures, such as but not limited to body cavity searches or executions by lethal injections, performed solely for correctional purposes and without informed consent.

Nursing Practice in Correctional Settings

Correctional health care is one of the fastest growing specialties in health services today and offers new and unique roles for nursing in the evolving correctional healthcare settings. Because healthcare services are offered within community corrections facilities, jails, juvenile detention centers, and both juvenile and adult correctional institutions, the registered nurse must be prepared to address a wide spectrum of needs, including those associated with women's health, the pediatric through geriatric age continuum, and end-of-life care of patients in corrections settings. Such corrections facilities can house fewer than 50 juveniles or adults, or thousands of adult inmates. The majority of large adult correctional systems have one or more specialized facilities.

Most detainees do not need frequent or ongoing nursing care, and the registered nurse is not usually involved in assisting with activities of daily living except for those services required in infirmaries, skilled nursing or extended care areas or facilities, and hospital settings. Almost all adult incarcerated offenders need at least occasional nursing services for the treatment of injuries, flu symptoms, back pain, headache, etc. Many also need nursing evaluations subsequent to altercations with other inmates, use of force, segregation placement, mental health crises, and/or other such intermittent circumstances.

Nurses usually interact with inmates in clinic areas or inmate housing units, but they may need to provide emergency care for patients in both indoor and outdoor work sites, recreational facilities, classrooms, dining facilities, visiting rooms, and other common areas. Real-life examples of such emergent care instances reported by experienced corrections nurses include delivery of a baby in the women's shower, farm injuries (one inmate was gored by a boar, another was trampled by a steer, and another fell off a barn roof), and industrial injuries (one inmate got his fingers caught in a router, one cut off the tips of his fingers with a saw, another caught his hand in an ironing press, and another got metal splinters in his eye while working in a metal shop).

The major emphasis of nursing care in most correctional settings is the provision of primary care services for the juvenile or adult population. These services are comparable to the care and surveillance services requiring the skills characteristic of public health, community health, occupational health, ambulatory care, emergency, and school nurses. Clinical settings include outpatient and urgent care clinics, acute care, skilled nursing, and long-term care inpatient healthcare facilities. Primary health services include the provision of intake evaluations, health screenings, direct healthcare services, analyzing individual health behaviors, teaching, counseling, and assisting individuals in assuming responsibility for their own health to the best of their ability, knowledge, and circumstances. Specialized mental health and chemical dependency units and facilities, critical care, neurological trauma, and dialysis services may supplement the primary care resources and require appropriately prepared specialty registered nurses and advanced practice registered nurses.

Registered nurses, as the primary healthcare providers in correctional settings, are challenged to provide health education and health promotion activities, evaluate the effectiveness of planned care, encourage preventive behavior, and address other public health issues within the prison setting. In addition, the registered nurse coordinates the linkage to community heathcare resources prior to the offender's release from incarceration, a critical function that provides the inmate the opportunity for continuity of care and helps facilitate a successful return to the community.

General Nursing Practice

The needs of the correctional population demand that the corrections nurse have a sound background preparation in community/public health, psychiatric, emergency, disease management and chronic care, medical-surgical and, in some settings, critical care nursing. Skills in negotiation, problem solving, listening, and communication are invaluable.

The registered nurse in corrections must be able to demonstrate good assessment and organizational skills as well as critical decision-making and thinking skills, especially when serving in the role of the only healthcare provider on site. Facility protocols and provider-generated order sets provide direction for the healthcare activities and specific patient care measures. However, such structures do not allow the corrections nurse to abdicate one's professional nursing responsibility for appropriate assessment, critical thinking, decision-making, and patient advocacy activities.

The registered nurse, in addition to providing direct nursing care, assesses the patient's health status, analyzes the assessment data, develops or modifies diagnoses, develops or modifies the plan of care based on those assessments and diagnoses, and evaluates the effectiveness of the plan of care. The corrections nurse often cares for patients with multiple and complex health conditions and diagnoses requiring an increased intensity of healthcare resources. The necessary associated nursing activities include patient assessment; decisions about medication, treatment delivery, and assessment of their effects; crisis intervention; triage; education; and patient advocacy. Scheduling of appointments, transportation, and other resources may require complex planning and the negotiation of staff and fiscal resources.

Nursing care within the corrections setting may be provided in collaboration with other nurses and health professionals, or independently, which is most often the case in a small or rural facility. Nursing care may be provided by a team of nurses with differing levels of preparation and licensure, including the registered nurse, advanced practice registered nurse, and licensed practical nurse. The preferred educational preparation of the registered nurse for entry into corrections nursing practice is at the baccalaureate level. Continuing professional development is expected, including further educational preparation to achieve a baccalaureate or graduate-level degree.

Correctional facilities vary in size and configuration. The overriding mission of security, with its locks, cameras, bars, correctional officers, and searches creates an environment of noise, distractions, and confusion which must be appropriately managed to maintain a therapeutic environment for nursing care. For example, consider how medication administration by nurses differs in this non-healthcare environment. In corrections settings medication administration may be accomplished by what is referred to in some settings as a "pill line" where the patient comes to the medication area and receives the necessary therapy. Large numbers of patients and large numbers of medications or treatments may require that nurses negotiate care delivery and medication administration times and may also increase the potential for errors that result with interruptions and distractions. Such patient encounters may necessitate unscheduled time allocations for reassessment and educational intervention opportunities.

Nursing practice must be balanced with the goals of corrections and the incarcerated person's rights to appropriate health care. If the patient cannot present for healthcare services because of disability, injury, or seclusion restrictions, the corrections nurse must go to the patient's location, conduct an appropriate and timely assessment, render or secure appropriate healthcare services, and accurately complete the necessary documentation record(s). The published *Standards for Health Services in Correctional Institutions* of the American Public Health Association (APHA 2003), the American Correctional Association and the National Commission on Correctional Health Care standards, along with state laws and state nurse practice acts and regulations, can provide guidance and support for the corrections nurse.

Working inside a correctional setting requires that the corrections nurse have knowledge of the legal aspects of nursing and litigation related to correctional health care. The corrections nurse must be acutely aware of the need for appropriate documentation of care rendered. Maintaining confidentiality of patient health information often requires special attention, especially when corrections staff must assist in monitoring the health status of patients.

The corrections nurse is expected to demonstrate integrity and highly ethical and moral practice, appreciating the legally mandated obligation to deliver nursing care regardless of the individual's circumstances or offenses. The basic concept of patient advocacy may be foreign to the corrections environment and may need to be regularly reaffirmed by the corrections nurse.

The licensed practical or vocational nurse, in accordance with the licensure laws of the state and under the direction of a registered nurse or advanced practice clinician, provides basic nursing care, collaborates with other members of the healthcare team in the development and implementation of a nursing plan of care, and contributes to an evaluation of the effectiveness of that plan.

Advanced Practice Registered Nurse

The advanced practice registered nurse (APRN) roles include the clinical nurse specialist (CNS), nurse practitioner (NP), certified nurse midwife (CNM), and certified registered nurse anesthetist (CRNA). The APRN guides the practice and critical thinking of nursing and other healthcare personnel, carries out advanced clinical practice activities, manages one or more clinical practice settings, incorporates scientific knowledge from other disciplines into practice and management, and evaluates the health care provided in those settings through a comprehensive quality assurance system. In the corrections environment, the CNS, NP, or CNM with prescriptive authority often serves as the sole primary care provider. Fewer practice opportunities are currently available for the CRNA. The APRN's practice is characterized by the depth and breadth of knowledge in a nursing specialty and the ability to incorporate knowledge of the correctional field in planning, implementing, and managing health care.

Role Specialty Practice

Corrections nurses may engage in role specialty practice when their primary efforts are focused on education, discharge planning, case management, or administration. Their work most often requires a systems perspective and incorporates fiscal and regulatory considerations in decision-making.

The education and knowledge base acquired at the baccalaureate and master's level prepares corrections nurses to function in administrative roles such as health services managers and chief nurse administrators for large systems. Their clinical expertise, combined with their administrative and managerial training, gives these nurse leaders the depth and breadth of preparation to serve at the senior executive and manager levels to address the inherent political and organizational complexities of the correctional healthcare delivery system.

Educational Preparation and Specialty Certification

Corrections nursing curriculum content and associated clinical practicum experiences are rarely incorporated in formal academic programs at the undergraduate nursing level. If included, most often guest faculty are invited to address care of such vulnerable populations during community health courses. A similar paucity of specific corrections nursing content and specialty practice opportunities characterizes the graduate level educational programs, especially for those preparing registered nurses for the advanced practice roles of clinical nurse specialist, nurse practitioner, and certified nurse midwife. Some academic nursing programs have recently initiated discussions about strategies to formally integrate corrections nursing content or tracks within existing or future curricula.

Nurses interested in the corrections environment may find additional learning opportunities available in college-level criminal justice courses and continuing education and certificate programs offered by such organizations as the American Correctional Association (ACA) and the National Commission on Correctional Health Care (NCCHC). Corrections nurses may also elect to expand their skills and knowledge in other clinical specialty programs of interest such as pediatric, psychiatric–mental health, oncology, hospice and palliative care, or gerontology nursing. Formal preparation for nursing administration roles may be achieved through completion of a graduate-level program in nursing administration. Others may elect to seek advanced degrees in business administration, economics, finance, or law to complement their nursing education preparation and experience.

Certification and advanced certification in correctional health are available through the National Commission on Correctional Health Care. This organization identifies the two types of certification as CCHP for entry level and CCHP-A for the advanced level.

In 2006 the American Correctional Association established a certification program for corrections nurses. ACA's Corrections Certification Program is offered in two specialty categories: Certified Corrections Nurse Manager (CCN/M) and Certified Corrections Nurse (CCN).

Certification in nursing administration and other nursing specialties is available through the American Nurses Credentialing Center (ANCC) and other certification bodies. Other certification and credentialing processes may also be recommended or required for specific corrections settings.

Ethics

The registered nurse in the corrections environment is bound by the profession's *Code of Ethics for Nurses with Interpretive Statements* (ANA 2001).

The privacy provision of the Health Insurance Portability and Accountability Act (HIPAA) of 1996 became mandatory in 2003 and has been applied in correctional healthcare systems. Correctional facilities are struggling to determine the relevance and applicability of HIPAA to their operations. Although few state systems have the funds available to support compliance (Orr & Helderstein 2002), the corrections nurse must continue to assure confidentiality and security of patient information, and also advocate for patient privacy as appropriate. Such special regulatory and administrative mandates may create tension as the realities of insufficient fiscal and personnel resources conflict with the rights of the prisoner. For example, medication management and administration may be the responsibility of the guards and other security staff, rather than that of the registered nurse.

By the nature of the practice environment, corrections nurses must consider the primary importance of maintaining public safety. Security issues and concerns are paramount within the correctional institution. Nurses work in partnership with security and correctional staff to assure the provision of appropriate health care to confined individuals. The focus of maintaining security makes correctional nursing practice unique and dynamic, requiring a careful balance of priorities. For example, the person with acute asthma may need immediate access to appropriate inhaler medications to effectively manage their disease. Modifications to the plan of care must be made for the newly diagnosed diabetic patient who needs to learn how to manage their insulin therapy, when needles and syringes cannot be within their assigned berthing area.

The maintenance of professional boundaries is essential in the corrections environment. The nurse must act in the best interest of the patient's medical condition while maintaining a safe and secure environment. Those who cross professional boundaries place themselves, their peers, and others, including the patient, in a position of compromised security and personal safety. These and numerous other issues may merit an ethics consult.

Trends and Issues in Corrections Nursing

Corrections nurses must be advocates for maintaining good conditions of confinement by meeting national standards and monitoring basic needs of daily living in the corrections environment. Constant monitoring of infectious diseases, such as tuberculosis, HIV/AIDS, and hepatitis, in the corrections setting is an important process. Education and prevention become a public health obligation for the corrections nurse in preventing the spread and enhancing the treatment of these infectious diseases in the corrections staff assigned to the facility. This becomes even more important when the incarcerated individual returns to the community and has not yet been cured.

The constitutional right to health care and the changing of community standards of care need to be considered by corrections nurses when developing and reviewing policies in the corrections setting. Research and current practice trends need to be consulted and integrated when appropriate. For example, research supports the use of treatment modalities based on cognitive restructuring to change antisocial behaviors for the corrections populations. These new approaches have significant implications for the corrections nurse working with an aging population, increased numbers of the chronically mentally ill, increased numbers of incarcerated women, and individuals with drug and alcohol abuse.

The increasing numbers of special needs patients, such as those who are chronically ill, elderly, or terminally ill, raise organizational and facility issues that must be addressed. Should elderly and infirm inmates be housed in a separate care setting or be mainstreamed with younger, active, and possibly more aggressive inmates? Prisons are not designed or staffed to provide sophisticated and intensive care for large numbers of chronically ill people. Do new or renovated corrections facilities need to be designed to easily accommodate those with disabilities, such as visual or auditory deficits, or those who are wheelchair-bound or dependent on other mobility assistance?

The managed-care environment is part of corrections nursing. The significant trend of notable budget cuts for health care of inmates is reflective of current times. The frontline corrections nurse manager is charged with maintaining medically necessary care with limited budgetary resources. Nurses are encouraged to uphold the intrinsic values of quality nursing care and to take action if these values are compromised.

The application of telehealth technology has become an enhancement for delivery of healthcare services in the corrections environment. The maintenance of public safety by decreasing movement of patients outside the correctional facility and the practical aspects of making specialist care more readily accessible to more individuals has made the correctional settings a perfect venue for telehealth. This technology solution requires corrections nurses to expand their competencies and knowledge base and also address the resulting documentation and confidentiality issues.

Recruitment and retention of nurses is a challenge for chief nursing officers (CNOs) and administrators in any healthcare setting. This traditional challenge has an even greater impact for the specialty of corrections nursing. Corrections nursing, with its focus on special populations in remote and poorly resourced settings, continues to challenge those desiring to practice in these environments. The pay scale in these settings is often far behind that offered in larger urban settings. Without the recognition and inclusion of corrections nurses in mainstream nursing initiatives, few opportunities exist for nurses to learn about specialization in this area. These challenges can be minimized as corrections nurses align themselves within their specialty and within the larger nursing and healthcare communities. This level of engagement promotes visibility, educates, and bridges the connections between correctional, public, and community health specialties.

Alternative healthcare delivery models include reliance on contracted services of outside agencies rather than department of corrections employees. Because of constraints imposed by mandated bureaucratic county and state hiring practices and set salary scales, these contractors are more successful in recruiting staff to remote areas avoided by nurses and other healthcare professionals. Privatization of inmate healthcare services has the advantage of adjusting salaries to match local wages, providing flexibility to adjust schedules and share staff positions, and hiring temporary staff in times of increased workloads. However, because of the inherent security concerns prevalent in correctional facilities, all nurses require an in-depth orientation to their job assignment, infection control issues, and the security aspects of the institution.

Summary

The corrections nursing specialty allows registered nurses to practice nursing with the compassion and integrity that reflects the essence of nursing. Corrections nurses develop and use strong clinical skills and critical thinking as they manage and respond quickly and decisively when working with this vulnerable population. Nurses utilize their clinical competence, professionalism, and excellent communication skills to deliver high-quality care. Autonomy and independence characterize this practice. The corrections nurse uses negotiation skills that permit positive interactions and effective dialogue with patients and staff in the correctional setting. Such positive interaction allows the nurse to respect the corrections goal of security while promoting patient advocacy and health for this population. Nurses must deliver care in an unbiased and nonjudgmental manner in this challenging environment.

Standards of Corrections Nursing Practice
Standards of Practice

The corrections nurse is a registered nurse working in a corrections environment or with confined or detained individuals.

Standard 1. Assessment
The corrections nurse collects comprehensive data pertinent to the patient's health and condition or the situation.

Measurement Criteria:

The corrections nurse:

- Collects data in a systematic and ongoing process.

- Involves the patient, family, and other healthcare and community providers and agencies, as appropriate, in holistic data collection.

- Prioritizes data collection activities based on the patient's immediate condition, the environment of care, and anticipated needs of the patient or situation.

- Uses appropriate evidence-based assessment techniques and instruments in collecting pertinent data.

- Uses analytical models and problem-solving tools.

- Synthesizes available data, information, and knowledge relevant to the situation to identify patterns and variances.

- Documents relevant data in a retrievable format.

Additional Measurement Criteria for the Advanced Practice Registered Nurse:

The advanced practice registered nurse:

- Initiates and interprets diagnostic tests and procedures relevant to the patient's current status.

Standard 2. Diagnosis
The corrections nurse analyzes the assessment data to determine the diagnoses or issues.

Measurement Criteria:

The corrections nurse:

- Derives the diagnoses or related issues based on assessment data.
- Validates the diagnoses or issues with the patient, family, and other healthcare and community providers when possible and appropriate.
- Documents diagnoses or issues in a manner that facilitates the determination of the expected outcomes and plan.

Additional Measurement Criteria for the Advanced Practice Registered Nurse:

The advanced practice registered nurse:

- Systematically compares clinical findings with normal and abnormal variations and developmental events in formulating a differential diagnosis.
- Utilizes complex data and information obtained during interview, examination, and diagnostic procedures in determining diagnoses.
- Assists staff in developing and maintaining competency in the diagnostic process.

STANDARD 3. OUTCOMES IDENTIFICATION
The corrections nurse identifies expected outcomes for a plan individualized to the patient or the situation.

Measurement Criteria:

The corrections nurse:

- Involves the patient, family, and other healthcare and community providers and agencies in formulating expected outcomes when possible and appropriate.

- Derives culturally appropriate expected outcomes from the diagnoses.

- Considers associated risks, security issues, benefits, costs, current scientific evidence, and clinical expertise when formulating expected outcomes.

- Defines expected outcomes in terms of the patient, patient values, ethical considerations, environment, and situation considering associated risks, security issues, benefits and costs, and current scientific evidence.

- Includes a time estimate for attainment of expected outcomes.

- Develops expected outcomes that provide direction for continuity of care.

- Modifies expected outcomes based on changes in the status of the patient or evaluation of the situation.

- Documents expected outcomes as measurable goals.

Additional Measurement Criteria for the Advanced Practice Registered Nurse:

The advanced practice registered nurse:

- Identifies expected outcomes that incorporate cost and clinical effectiveness, patient acceptance, and continuity and consistency among providers.

- Supports the use of clinical guidelines linked to positive patient outcomes.

STANDARD 4. PLANNING

The corrections nurse develops a plan that prescribes strategies and alternatives to attain expected outcomes.

Measurement Criteria:

The corrections nurse:

- Develops an individualized plan considering patient characteristics and the situation (e.g., age, gender, cultural appropriateness, environmental sensitivity).

- Develops the plan in conjunction with the patient, family, community and public health resources, security personnel, and others, as appropriate.

- Includes strategies in the plan that address each of the identified diagnoses or issues, which may include strategies for promotion and restoration of health and prevention of illness, injury, and disease.

- Provides for continuity of care within the plan.

- Incorporates an implementation pathway or time line within the plan.

- Establishes the plan priorities with the patient, family, security personnel, and others as appropriate.

- Utilizes the plan to provide direction to other members of the healthcare team and the security personnel.

- Defines the plan to reflect current statutes, rules and regulations, guidelines, and standards.

- Integrates current trends and research affecting care in the planning process.

- Considers the economic impact of the plan.

- Uses standardized language or recognized terminology to document the plan.

Additional Measurement Criteria for the Advanced Practice Registered Nurse:

The advanced practice registered nurse:

- Includes assessment, diagnostic strategies, and therapeutic interventions in the plan that reflect current evidence, including data, research, literature, and expert clinical knowledge.

- Selects or designs strategies to meet the multifaceted needs of complex patients.

- Includes the synthesis of the patient's values and beliefs regarding nursing and medical therapies in the plan.

Additional Measurement Criteria for the Nursing Role Specialty:

The corrections nurse in a nursing role specialty:

- Participates in the design and development of multidisciplinary, interdisciplinary, and interagency processes to address the situation or issue.

- Contributes to the development and continuous improvement of organizational systems that support the planning process.

- Supports the integration of clinical, human, financial, and security resources to enhance and complete the decision-making processes.

Standard 5. Implementation
The corrections nurse implements the identified plan.

Measurement Criteria:

The corrections nurse:

• Implements the plan in a safe and timely manner.

• Documents implementation and any modifications, including changes or omissions, of the identified plan.

• Utilizes evidence-based interventions and treatments specific to the diagnosis or problem.

• Utilizes corrections facility and community resources and systems to implement the plan.

• Collaborates with nursing colleagues, healthcare team members, security personnel, and others to implement the plan.

Additional Measurement Criteria for the Advanced Practice Registered Nurse:

The advanced practice registered nurse:

• Supports collaboration with healthcare colleagues, security personnel, and other disciplines to implement the plan.

• Incorporates new knowledge and strategies to initiate change in healthcare practices if desired outcomes are not achieved.

Additional Measurement Criteria for the Nursing Role Specialty:

The corrections nurse in a nursing role specialty:

• Facilitates utilization of systems and community resources to implement the plan.

• Implements the plan using principles and concepts of project or systems management.

• Fosters organizational systems that support implementation of the plan.

STANDARD 5A. COORDINATION OF CARE
The corrections nurse coordinates care delivery.

Measurement Criteria:

The corrections nurse:

- Coordinates implementation of the plan.
- Employs strategies to promote health and a safe and secure environment.
- Documents the coordination of care.

Measurement Criteria for the Advanced Practice Registered Nurse:

The advanced practice registered nurse:

- Provides leadership in the coordination of multidisciplinary health care for integrated delivery of patient care services.
- Synthesizes data and information in order to prescribe necessary system and community support measures, including environmental modifications.
- Coordinates system and community resources that enhance delivery of care across continuums.

Measurement Criteria for the Nurse in the Role Specialty:

The corrections nurse in a nursing role specialty:

- Coordinates system and community resources that enhance delivery of care across continuums.
- Evaluates fiscal impact and needs when making decisions related to the delivery of care.

STANDARD 5B. HEALTH TEACHING AND HEALTH PROMOTION
The corrections nurse employs strategies to promote health and a safe environment.

Measurement Criteria:

The corrections nurse:

- Provides health teaching to patients, family, colleagues, and security personnel that addresses such topics as healthy lifestyles, risk-reducing behaviors, developmental needs, activities of daily living, and preventive self-care.

- Uses health promotion and health teaching methods appropriate to the situation and the patient's developmental level, learning needs, readiness, ability to learn, language preference, and culture.

- Seeks opportunities for feedback and evaluation of the effectiveness of the strategies used.

Additional Measurement Criteria for the Advanced Practice Registered Nurse:

The advanced practice registered nurse:

- Synthesizes empirical evidence on risk behaviors, epidemiology, and other related theories and frameworks when designing health information and patient education.

- Designs patient education appropriate to the patient's developmental level, learning needs, readiness to learn, and cultural values and beliefs.

Additional Measurement Criteria for the Nursing Role Specialty:

The corrections nurse in a nursing role specialty:

- Synthesizes empirical evidence on risk behaviors, learning theories, behavioral change theories, motivational theories, epidemiology, and other related theories and frameworks when designing health information and patient education.

- Designs health information and patient education appropriate to the patient's developmental level, learning needs, readiness to learn, and cultural values and beliefs.

- Designs, implements, and supports health teaching that addresses chronic illness, communicable disease, access to health care, and emergency care specific for the corrections environment.

- Evaluates health information resources, such as the Internet, within the area of practice for accuracy, readability, and comprehensibility to help patients access quality health information.

STANDARD 5C. CONSULTATION

The advanced practice registered nurse and the nursing role specialist provide consultation to influence the identified plan, enhance the abilities of others, and effect change.

Measurement Criteria for the Advanced Practice Registered Nurse:

The advanced practice registered nurse:

- Synthesizes clinical data, theoretical frameworks, and evidence when providing consultation.

- Facilitates the effectiveness of a consultation by involving the patient in decision making and negotiating role responsibilities.

- Communicates consultation recommendations that facilitate change.

Measurement Criteria for the Nursing Role Specialty:

The corrections nurse in a nursing role specialty:

- Synthesizes data, information, theoretical frameworks, and evidence when providing consultation.

- Facilitates the effectiveness of a consultation by involving the stakeholders in the decision-making process.

- Communicates consultation recommendations that influence the identified plan, facilitate understanding by involved stakeholders, enhance the work of others, and effect change.

STANDARD 5D. PRESCRIPTIVE AUTHORITY AND TREATMENT

The advanced practice registered nurse uses prescriptive authority, procedures, referrals, treatments, and therapies in accordance with state and federal laws and regulations.

Measurement Criteria for the Advanced Practice Registered Nurse:

The advanced practice registered nurse:

- Prescribes evidence-based treatments, therapies, and procedures considering the patient's comprehensive healthcare needs.

- Prescribes pharmacological agents based on a current knowledge of pharmacology and physiology.

- Prescribes specific pharmacological agents and treatments based on clinical indicators, the patient's status and needs, and the results of diagnostic and laboratory tests.

- Evaluates therapeutic and potential adverse effects of pharmacological and non-pharmacological treatments.

- Provides patients with information about intended effects and potential adverse effects of proposed prescriptive therapies.

- Provides information about costs and alternative treatments and procedures, as appropriate.

STANDARD 6. EVALUATION
The corrections nurse evaluates progress towards attainment of outcomes.

Measurement Criteria:

The corrections nurse:

- Conducts a systematic, ongoing, and criterion-based evaluation of the outcomes in relation to the structures and processes prescribed by the plan and the indicated time line.

- Includes the patient and others involved in the care or situation in the evaluative process.

- Evaluates the effectiveness of the planned strategies in relation to patient responses and the attainment of the expected outcomes.

- Documents the results of the evaluation.

- Uses ongoing assessment data to revise the diagnoses, outcomes, plan, and implementation as needed.

- Disseminates the results to the patient and others involved in the care or situation, as appropriate, in accordance with state and federal laws and regulations.

Additional Measurement Criteria for the Advanced Practice Registered Nurse:

The advanced practice registered nurse:

- Evaluates the accuracy of the diagnosis and effectiveness of the interventions in relation to the patient's attainment of expected outcomes.

- Synthesizes the results of the evaluation analyses to determine the impact of the plan on the affected patients, families, groups, communities, and corrections and other institutions.

- Uses the results of the evaluation analyses to make or recommend process or structural changes including policy, procedure, or protocol documentation, as appropriate.

Additional Measurement Criteria for the Nursing Role Specialty:

The corrections nurse in a nursing role specialty:

- Uses the results of the evaluation analyses to make or recommend process or structural changes, including policy, procedure, regulation, and legislation, or protocol documentation, as appropriate.

- Synthesizes the results of the evaluation analyses to determine the impact of the plan on the affected patients, families, groups, communities, and corrections and other institutions, networks, and organizations.

Standards of Professional Performance

The corrections nurse is a registered nurse working in a corrections environment or with confined or detained individuals.

Standard 7. Quality of Practice
The corrections nurse systematically enhances the quality and effectiveness of nursing practice.

Measurement Criteria:

The corrections nurse:

- Demonstrates quality by documenting the application of the nursing process in a responsible, accountable, and ethical manner.

- Uses creativity and innovation in nursing practice to improve care delivery.

- Incorporates new knowledge to initiate changes in nursing practice if desired outcomes are not achieved.

- Participates in quality improvement activities. Such activities may include:

  - Identifying aspects of practice important for quality monitoring.

  - Using indicators developed to monitor quality and effectiveness of nursing practice.

  - Collecting data to monitor quality and effectiveness of nursing practice.

  - Analyzing quality data to identify opportunities for improving nursing practice.

  - Formulating recommendations to improve nursing practice or outcomes.

  - Implementing activities to enhance the quality of nursing practice.

  - Developing, implementing, and evaluating policies, procedures, and guidelines to improve the quality of practice.

Continued ▶

- Participating on interdisciplinary teams to evaluate clinical care or health services.
- Participating in efforts to minimize costs and unnecessary duplication.
- Analyzing factors related to safety, satisfaction, effectiveness, and cost–benefit options.
- Analyzing organizational systems for barriers.
- Implementing processes that promote optimal, safe, and effective care.
- Uses the results of quality improvement activities to initiate changes in nursing practice, healthcare delivery, and the correctional system.

Additional Measurement Criteria for the Advanced Practice Registered Nurse:

The advanced practice registered nurse:

- Obtains and maintains professional certification if available in the area of expertise.
- Designs quality improvement initiatives.
- Implements initiatives to evaluate the need for change.
- Evaluates the practice environment and quality of nursing care rendered in relation to existing evidence, identifying opportunities for the generation and use of research.

Additional Measurement Criteria for the Nursing Role Specialty:

The corrections nurse in a nursing role specialty:

- Obtains and maintains professional certification if available in the area of expertise.
- Designs quality improvement initiatives.
- Implements initiatives to evaluate the need for change.
- Evaluates the practice environment, including the quality of nursing care, in relation to existing evidence, identifying opportunities for improvement, including the generation and use of research.

STANDARD 8. EDUCATION

The corrections nurse attains knowledge and competency that reflects current nursing practice.

Measurement Criteria:

The corrections nurse:

- Participates in ongoing educational activities related to appropriate knowledge bases and professional issues.

- Demonstrates a commitment to lifelong learning through self-reflection and inquiry to identify learning needs.

- Seeks experiences that reflect current practice in order to maintain skills and competence in clinical practice or role performance.

- Acquires knowledge and skills appropriate to the specialty area, practice setting, role, or situation.

- Maintains professional records that provide evidence of competency and lifelong learning.

- Seeks experiences and formal and independent learning activities to maintain and develop clinical and professional skills and knowledge.

Additional Measurement Criteria for the Advanced Practice Registered Nurse:

The advanced practice registered nurse:

- Uses current healthcare research findings and other evidence to expand clinical knowledge, enhance role performance, and increase knowledge of professional issues.

Additional Measurement Criteria for the Nursing Role Specialty:

The corrections nurse in a nursing role specialty:

- Uses current research findings and other evidence to expand knowledge, enhance role performance, and increase knowledge of professional and leadership issues.

STANDARD 9. PROFESSIONAL PRACTICE EVALUATION

The corrections nurse evaluates one's own nursing practice in relation to professional practice standards and guidelines, relevant statutes, rules, and regulations.

Measurement Criteria:

The corrections nurse's practice reflects the application of knowledge of current practice standards, guidelines, statutes, rules, and regulations.

The corrections nurse:

- Provides nursing care considering age, culture, ethnicity, and the unique aspects of the correctional environment.

- Engages in self-evaluation of practice on a regular basis, identifying areas of strength as well as areas in which professional development would be beneficial.

- Obtains informal feedback regarding one's own practice from patients, peers, professional colleagues, and others.

- Participates in systematic peer review as appropriate.

- Takes action to achieve goals identified during the evaluation process.

- Provides rationales for practice beliefs, decisions, and actions as part of the informal and formal evaluation processes.

Additional Measurement Criteria for the Advanced Practice Registered Nurse:

The advanced practice registered nurse:

- Engages in a formal process seeking feedback regarding one's own practice from patients, peers, professional colleagues, and others.

Additional Measurement Criteria for the Nursing Role Specialty:

The corrections nurse in a nursing role specialty:

- Engages in a formal process seeking feedback regarding role performance from individuals; professional colleagues; representatives and administrators of corrections, government, or corporate entities; and others.

STANDARD 10. COLLEGIALITY
The corrections nurse interacts with and contributes to the professional development of peers and colleagues.

Measurement Criteria:

The corrections nurse:

- Shares knowledge and skills with peers and colleagues as evidenced by such activities as patient care conferences or presentations at formal or informal meetings.
- Provides peers with feedback regarding their practice and role performance.
- Interacts with peers and colleagues to enhance one's own professional nursing practice and role performance.
- Maintains compassionate and caring relationships with peers and colleagues.
- Contributes to an environment that is conducive to the education of healthcare professionals.
- Contributes to a supportive and healthy work environment.

Additional Measurement Criteria for the Advanced Practice Registered Nurse:

The advanced practice registered nurse:

- Models expert practice to interdisciplinary team members and healthcare consumers.
- Mentors and precepts other corrections nurses and colleagues as appropriate.
- Participates with interdisciplinary teams that contribute to role development and advanced nursing practice and health care.

Additional Measurement Criteria for the Nursing Role Specialty:

The corrections nurse in a nursing role specialty:

- Participates on multidisciplinary teams that contribute to role development and, directly or indirectly, advance nursing practice and health services.
- Mentors and precepts other corrections nurses and colleagues, as appropriate.

Standards of Professional Performance

STANDARD 11. COLLABORATION
The corrections nurse collaborates with patient, family, and others in the conduct of nursing practice.

Measurement Criteria:

The corrections nurse:

- Communicates with patient, family, healthcare providers, and corrections staff regarding patient care and the nurse's role in the provision of that care.

- Collaborates in creating a documented plan focused on outcomes and decisions related to care and delivery of services that indicates communication with patients, families, and others.

- Partners with others to effect change and generate positive outcomes through knowledge of the patient or situation.

- Documents referrals, including provisions for continuity of care.

Additional Measurement Criteria for the Advanced Practice Registered Nurse:

The advanced practice registered nurse:

- Partners with other disciplines to enhance patient care through interdisciplinary activities such as education, consultation, management, technological development, and research opportunities.

- Facilitates an interdisciplinary process with other members of the healthcare team.

- Documents plan of care communications, rationales for plan of care changes, and collaborative discussions to improve patient care.

Additional Measurement Criteria for Nursing Role Specialty:

The corrections nurse in a nursing role specialty:

- Works with others to enhance health care, and ultimately patient care, through interdisciplinary activities such as education, consultation, management, technological development, and research opportunities.

- Facilitates an interdisciplinary process with corrections staff and community resources.

- Documents plans, communications, rationales for plan changes, and collaborative discussions.

STANDARD 12. ETHICS
The corrections nurse integrates ethical provisions in all areas of practice.

Measurement Criteria:

The corrections nurse:

- Uses *Code of Ethics for Nurses with Interpretive Statements* (ANA 2001) to guide practice.

- Delivers care in a manner that preserves and protects patient autonomy, dignity, and rights.

- Maintains patient confidentiality within legal and regulatory parameters considering the unique corrections environment.

- Serves as a patient advocate and assists patients in developing skills for self-advocacy.

- Maintains a therapeutic and professional patient–nurse relationship with appropriate professional role boundaries.

- Demonstrates a commitment to practicing self-care, managing stress, and connecting with self and others.

- Contributes to resolving ethical issues of patients, colleagues, or systems as evidenced in such activities as participating on ethics committees.

- Reports illegal, incompetent, or impaired practices.

Additional Measurement Criteria for the Advanced Practice Registered Nurse:

The advanced practice registered nurse:

- Informs the patient of the risks, benefits, and outcomes of health-care regimens.

- Participates in interdisciplinary teams that address ethical risks, benefits, and outcomes.

Additional Measurement Criteria for the Nursing Role Specialty:

The corrections nurse in a nursing role specialty:

- Participates in multidisciplinary and interdisciplinary teams that address ethical risks, benefits, and outcomes.

- Informs administrators or others of the risks, benefits, and outcomes of programs and decisions that affect healthcare delivery.

STANDARD 13. RESEARCH
The corrections nurse integrates research findings into practice.

Measurement Criteria:

The corrections nurse:

- Utilizes the best available evidence, including research findings, to guide practice decisions.

- Actively participates in research activities at various levels appropriate to the nurse's level of education and position. Such activities may include:

  - Identifying clinical problems specific to nursing research (patient care and nursing practice);

  - Participating in data collection (surveys, pilot projects, formal studies);

  - Participating in a formal committee or program;

  - Sharing research activities or findings with peers and others;

  - Conducting research;

  - Critically analyzing and interpreting research for application to practice;

  - Using research findings in the development of policies, procedures, and standards of practice in patient care; and

  - Incorporating research as a basis for learning.

- Recognizes the unique requirements of human subjects' protection in the corrections environment.

Additional Measurement Criteria for the Advanced Practice Registered Nurse:

The advanced practice registered nurse:

- Contributes to nursing knowledge by conducting or synthesizing research that discovers, examines, and evaluates knowledge, theories, criteria, and creative approaches to improve healthcare practice, especially in the corrections environment.

- Formally disseminates research findings through activities such as presentations, publications, consultation, and journal clubs.

Additional Measurement Criteria for the Nursing Role Specialty:

The corrections nurse in a nursing role specialty:

- Contributes to nursing knowledge by conducting or synthesizing research that discovers, examines, and evaluates knowledge, theories, criteria, and creative approaches to improve health care.

- Formally disseminates research findings through activities such as presentations, publications, consultation, and journal clubs.

STANDARD 14. RESOURCE UTILIZATION

The corrections nurse considers factors related to safety, effectiveness, cost, benefits, and impact on practice in the planning and delivery of nursing services.

Measurement Criteria:

The corrections nurse:

- Evaluates factors such as safety, security, effectiveness, availability, cost and benefits, efficiencies, and impact on practice when choosing practice options that would result in the same expected outcome.

- Assists the patient, family, corrections staff, and community resource personnel in identifying and securing appropriate and available services to address health-related needs.

- Assigns or delegates tasks, based on the needs and condition of the patient, potential for harm, stability of the patient's condition, complexity of the task, and predictability of the outcome.

- Assists the patient and family in becoming informed consumers about the options, risks, and benefits of treatment and care.

Additional Measurement Criteria for the Advanced Practice Registered Nurse:

The advanced practice registered nurse:

- Utilizes organizational and community resources to formulate multidisciplinary or interdisciplinary plans of care.

- Develops innovative solutions for patient care problems that address effective resource utilization and maintenance of quality.

- Develops evaluation strategies to demonstrate cost-effectiveness, cost–benefit, and efficiency factors associated with clinical practice.

Additional Measurement Criteria for the Nursing Role Specialty:

The corrections nurse in a nursing role specialty:

- Develops innovative solutions and applies strategies to obtain appropriate resources for nursing initiatives.

- Secures organizational resources to ensure a work environment conducive to completing the identified plan and outcomes.

- Develops evaluation methods to measure safety, security, and effectiveness for interventions and outcomes.

- Promotes activities that assist others, as appropriate, in becoming informed about costs, risks, and benefits of care or of the plan and treatment strategies.

STANDARD 15. LEADERSHIP
The corrections nurse provides leadership in the professional practice setting and the profession.

Measurement Criteria:

The corrections nurse:

- Engages in teamwork as a team player and a team builder.

- Works to create and maintain healthy work environments in local, regional, national, or international communities.

- Displays the ability to define a clear vision, associated goals, and a plan to implement and measure progress.

- Demonstrates a commitment to continuous, lifelong learning for self and others.

- Teaches others to succeed, by mentoring and other strategies.

- Exhibits creativity and flexibility through times of change.

- Demonstrates energy, excitement, and a passion for quality work.

- Willingly accepts mistakes by self and others, thereby creating a culture in which risk-taking is not only safe, but expected.

- Inspires loyalty through valuing of people as the most precious assets in an organization.

- Directs the coordination of care across settings and among caregivers, including oversight of licensed and unlicensed personnel in any assigned or delegated tasks.

- Serves in key roles in the work setting by participating in committees, councils, and administrative teams.

- Promotes advancement of the profession through participation in professional organizations.

Additional Measurement Criteria for the Advanced Practice Registered Nurse:

The advanced practice registered nurse:

- Works to influence decision-making bodies to improve patient care.

- Provides direction to enhance the effectiveness of the healthcare team.

- Initiates and revises protocols or guidelines to reflect evidence-based practice, to reflect accepted changes in care management, or to address emerging problems.

- Promotes communication of information and advancement of the profession through writing, publishing, and presentations for professional or lay audiences.

- Designs innovations to effect change in practice and improve health outcomes.

Additional Measurement Criteria for the Nursing Role Specialty:

The corrections nurse in a nursing role specialty:

- Works to influence decision-making bodies to improve patient care, health services, delivery systems, and organizational and governmental policies.

- Promotes communication of information and advancement of the profession through writing, publishing, and presentations for professional or lay audiences.

- Designs innovations to effect change in practice and outcomes.

- Provides direction to enhance the effectiveness of the multidisciplinary or interdisciplinary team.

Glossary

Assessment. A systematic, dynamic process by which the corrections nurse through interaction with the patient, family, groups, communities, public health agencies, populations, and healthcare providers, collects and analyzes data. Assessment may include the following dimensions: physical, psychological, sociocultural, spiritual, cognitive, functional abilities, developmental, economic, and lifestyle.

Caregiver. A person who provides direct care for another, such as a child, a dependent adult, or a person who is disabled or chronically ill.

Code of ethics. A list of provisions that makes explicit the primary goals, values, and obligations of the profession.

Community. Local health jurisdictions, health departments, hospitals, and similar entities; urgent care and emergency departments.

Continuity of care. An interdisciplinary process that includes patients, families, and significant others in the development of a coordinated plan of care. This process facilitates the patient's transition between settings and healthcare providers, based on changing needs and available resources.

Corrections environment. A facility or place of confinement that houses offender, detainee, or convicted clientele.

Corrections nurse. A registered nurse who works in a corrections environment or with confined or detained individuals.

Corrections nursing. The practice of nursing and the delivery of care within the unique and distinct environment of the criminal justice system. The criminal justice system includes jails, prisons, juvenile detention centers, substance abuse treatment facilities, and other facilities.

Criteria. Relevant, measurable indicators of the standards of practice and professional performance.

Data. Discrete entities that are described objectively without interpretation.

Diagnosis. A clinical judgment about the patient's response to actual or potential health conditions or needs. The diagnosis provides the basis for determination of a plan to achieve expected outcomes. Corrections nurses utilize nursing and/or medical diagnoses, depending upon educational and clinical preparation and legal authority.

Disease. A biological or psychosocial disorder of structure or function in a patient, especially one that produces specific signs or symptoms or that affects a specific part of the body, mind, or spirit.

Environment. The atmosphere, milieu, or conditions in which an individual lives, works, or plays.

Evaluation. The process of determining the progress toward attainment of expected outcomes, including the effectiveness of care, when addressing one's practice.

Evidence-based practice. A process founded on the collection, interpretation, and integration of valid, important, and applicable patient-reported, clinician-observed, and research-derived evidence. The best available evidence, moderated by patient circumstances and preferences, is applied to improve the quality of clinical judgments.

Expected outcomes. End results that are measurable, desirable, observable, and which translate into observable behaviors.

Family. Family of origin or significant others as identified by the patient.

Guidelines. Systematically developed statements that describe recommended actions based on available scientific evidence and expert opinion. Clinical guidelines describe a process of patient care management that has the potential of improving the quality of clinical and consumer decision making.

Health. An experience that is often expressed in terms of wellness and illness and which may occur in the presence or absence of disease or injury.

Healthcare providers. Individuals with special expertise who provide healthcare services or assistance to patients. They may include nurses, physicians, psychologists, social workers, nutritionists/dietitians, and various therapists.

Holistic. An understanding that the parts of a patient are intimately interconnected and that physical, mental, social, and spiritual factors need to be included in any interventions.

Illness. The subjective experience of discomfort.

Implementation. Activities such as teaching, monitoring, providing, counseling, delegating, and coordinating.

Information. Data that are interpreted, organized, or structured.

Interdisciplinary. Using the overlapping skills and knowledge of each team member and discipline resulting in synergistic effects where outcomes are enhanced and are more comprehensive than the simple aggregation of any team member's individual efforts.

Knowledge. Information that is synthesized so that relationships are identified and formalized.

Multidisciplinary. Using the contribution of discipline-specific skills by each team member or discipline.

Patient. Recipient of nursing practice. The term *patient* is used to provide consistency and brevity, bearing in mind that other terms such as client, individual, resident, family, groups, communities, or populations might be better choices in some instances. When the patient is an individual, the focus is on the health state, problems, or needs of the individual. When the patient is a family or group, the focus is on the health state of the unit as a whole or the reciprocal effects of the individual's health state on the other members of the unit. When the patient is a community or population, the focus is on personal and environmental health and the health risks of the community or population.

Peer review. A collegial, systematic, and periodic process by which health professionals are held accountable for practice and which fosters the refinement of one's knowledge, skills, and decision-making at all levels and in all areas of practice.

Plan. A comprehensive outline of the components that need to be addressed to attain expected outcomes.

Quality of care. The degree to which health services for patients, families, groups, communities, or populations increase the likelihood of desired outcomes and are consistent with current professional knowledge.

Situation. A set of circumstances, conditions, or events.

Stakeholders. Persons who are affected by and care about the outcome or situation; may include patients, families, communities, corrections staff, healthcare providers, and others.

Standard. An authoritative statement defined and promoted by the profession, by which the quality of practice, service, or education can be evaluated.

Strategy. A plan of action to achieve a major overall goal.

Time line. A chronology for the plan of action to achieve a major overall goal.

REFERENCES

American Correctional Association (ACA). 2004. Female offenders. [survey]. *Corrections Compendium 29*:(3). (May/June). White Plains, MD: ACA.

American Correctional Association. 2005a. *2005 Directory of adult and juvenile correctional departments, institutions, agencies, probation and parole authorities.* White Plains, MD: ACA.

American Correctional Association. 2005b. *Corrections Compendium 29*:(5). (September/October). White Plains, MD: ACA.

American Nurses Association (ANA). 2001. *Code of ethics for nurses with interpretive statements.* Washington, DC: American Nurses Publishing.

American Nurses Association (ANA). 2003. *Nursing's social policy statement, 2nd ed.* Washington, DC: Nursesbooks.org.

American Nurses Association (ANA). 2004. *Nursing: Scope and standards of practice.* Silver Spring, MD: Nursesbooks.org.

American Public Health Association (APHA). 2003. Standards for health services in correctional institutions. Washington, DC: APHA.

Anno, B. J. 1997. Health behaviors in prisons and correctional facilities, in *Handbook of health behaviors research, Vol. III: Demography, development, and diversity*, Ch. 14, ed. David S. Gochman. New York: Plenum Press.

Anno, B. J., C. Graham, J. E. Lawrence, & R. Shansky. 2004. *Correctional health care: Addressing the needs of elderly, chronically ill, and terminally ill inmates.* Washington, DC: Criminal Justice Institute, National Institute of Corrections. http://www.nicic.org/Downloads/PDF/2004/018735.pdf (accessed January 4, 2007).

Bureau of Justice Statistics. 2004. *Corrections statistics.* Washington, DC: Department of Justice. http://www.ojp.usdoj.gov/bjs/correct.htm (accessed January 4, 2007).

Estelle v. Gamble, 429 U.S. 97. 1976. Washington, DC: U.S. Supreme Court (available online). http://www.caselaw.lp.findlaw.com

Goldkuhle, U. 1999. Health service utilization by women in prison: Health needs indicators and response effects. *Journal of Correctional Health Care* 1:63–83.

Greenfeld, L. A., & T. L. Snell. 1999. Women offenders. Washington, DC: U.S. Dept of Justice, Bureau of Justice Statistics.

MacNeil, J. 2005. An Unanswered Health Disparity: TB Among Correctional Inmates: 1993–2003. *American Journal of Public Health* cited on www.medicalnewstoday.com/medicalnews.php?.newsid=31801 (accessed January 4, 2007).

Murtha, R. 1975. Changes in one city's system. *American Journal of Nursing* 75(3):421–22.

National Commission on Correctional Health Care (NCCHC). 2002. *The health status of soon-to-be-released inmates*. Washington, DC: NCCHC. http://www.ncchc.org/pubs/pubs_stbr.vol1.html (accessed January 4, 2007).

Orr, D., & D. Helderstein. 2002. HIPAA in state correctional systems. *Journal of Correctional Health Care* 9(3):345–59.

National Criminal Justice Reference Service. *Sourcebook of criminal justice statistics online, 31st ed.* 2003. Albany, NY: U.S. Dept. of Justice, Bureau of Justice Statistics, Hindelang Criminal Justice Research Center. http://www.albany.edu/sourcebook/ (accessed January 4, 2007).

U.S. Department of Health and Human Services (USDHHS). 2002. *The registered nurse population: Findings from the national sample survey of registered nurses, March 2000.* Washington, DC: USDHHS, Health Resource and Services Administration, Bureau of Health Professions, Division of Nursing. http://bhpr.hrsa.gov/healthworkforce/reports/rnsurvey/default.htm (accessed January 6, 2007).

U.S. Department of Justice (USDOJ). 2004. *Juvenile offenders and victims national report series.* http://www.ncjrs.gov/pdffiles1/ojjdp/202885.pdf (accessed January 4, 2007).

APPENDIX A.
Scope and Standards of Nursing Practice in Correctional Facilities (1995)

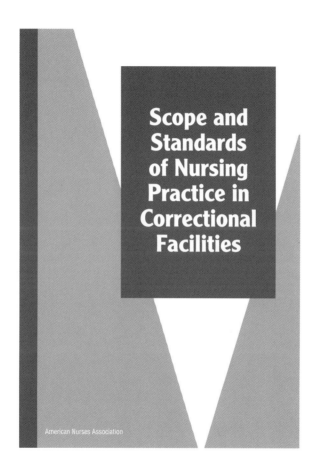

Scope and
Standards
of Nursing
Practice in
Correctional
Facilities

American Nurses Association

SCOPE and STANDARDS
of Nursing Practice
in Correctional Facilities

AMERICAN NURSES
ASSOCIATION

This document was developed by a Task Force chaired by Robert E. Myers, M.P.A., R.N., C.N.A.A., C.C.H.P., C.H.E., Member of the Board of Directors, American Correctional Health Services Association (ACHSA) and composed of ACHSA members with assistance from the Executive Committee on Community, Primary, and Long Term Care Nursing Practice, American Nurses Association. This document was adopted by the ANA Congress on Nursing Practice and the Board of Directors. The council gratefully acknowledges the assistance of those who contributed comments and recommendations during the field review process for this document.

Executive Committee, Council on Community, Primary, and Long Term Care Nursing Practice

LaVohn E. Josten, Ph.D., R.N., F.A.A.N., Chairperson
Cornelia M. Beck, Ph.D., R.N., F.A.A.N.

Joyce Newman Giger, Ed.D., R.N., C.S.
H. Marie McGrath, Ph.D., R.N.,C.
Margaret Edith Osborn, B.S.N., R.N.

Department of Practice, Economics and Policy Staff

Rita Munley Gallagher, Ph.D., R.N.,C., Senior Policy Fellow— Long Term Care
Patricia A. Rowell, Ph.D., R.N., Senior Policy Fellow— Standards and Guidelines

Victoria J. Boehm, B.G.S., Administrative Assistant

Published by
American Nurses Publishing
600 Maryland Avenue, SW
Suite 100 West
Washington, DC 20024-2571

NP-104   7.5M   6/95

CONTENTS

INTRODUCTION

The American Nurses Association (ANA) is responsible for defining the scope and standards of generic nursing practice. In 1991, ANA revised the standards of clinical nursing practice, broadening professional role expectations.[1] This document builds on those basic standards to delineate the scope and standards of clinical nursing practice in correctional facilities. The revised specialty standards also incorporate information from prior correctional health nursing standards.

Throughout history, nursing has been responsive to the ever-changing needs and demands for health care. Just as the practice of nursing is a dynamic, evolving process, so too is the process of defining the profession and the specialty areas within it. The *Scope and Standards of Nursing Practice in Correctional Facilities* is presented as the profession's guide to current correctional health nursing practice. This publication is intended to be used in conjunction with other documents that articulate the values of the nursing profession and the definition and scope of nursing practice.[2-7]

The standards apply to nurses in clinical practice across all correctional health settings and may be used in quality assurance programs as a means of evaluating and improving care. The standards are also a resource for assessment tools and plans of care, and may be used in the peer review and performance appraisal processes. Nurse colleagues and other professionals with an interest in correctional health will find this publication useful.

Within some standards, criteria are presented for two levels of professional nursing practice as defined in *Nursing: A Social Policy Statement*.[8] The roles of the basic and advanced practice nurse in correctional facilities are described in the scope statement in this document. The nurse who is prepared at the basic level provides care primarily to individuals and families and participates in the planning, implementation, and evaluation of nursing care. This nurse draws on the expertise of the advanced practice nurse. If an advanced practice nurse is not available, the nurse with basic preparation may assume some aspects of the advanced practice nurse's role, but the use of a consultant is recommended.

Advanced practice nurses, within their scope of practice, may perform all functions of the nurse who is prepared at the basic level. In addition, the advanced practice correctional health nurse has advanced education and substantial clinical experience with individuals, families, and groups; expertise in the formulation of health and social policy; and demonstrated proficiency in planning, implementing, and evaluating health programs.

As the specialty of correctional health nursing expands to meet increased demand, these standards and the description of the scope of correctional health nursing practice will require ongoing refinement. This document thus constitutes a challenge to correctional health nurses to provide quality care and to refine the scope and standards statement as the specialty evolves.

SCOPE OF NURSING PRACTICE IN CORRECTIONAL FACILITIES

Nursing is a dynamic, independent profession. In corrections, the nurse is frequently employed in an isolated environment where there is constant pressure to expand his or her scope of practice to meet new needs and demands. This unique environment can be stressful and antagonistic, and it may limit the range of available interventions. It may also require nurses to acknowledge their responsibility for providing only those services that fall within their legal practice parameters.

Nurses in correctional facilities provide health care to individuals incarcerated in jails, prisons, juvenile detention facilities, and similar settings. The populations incarcerated vary from youths to aged adults and include both women and men, from the healthy through the chronically ill, the mentally ill, and the developmentally disabled. In some settings, long term access to inmates facilitates planned care as well as the development of trusting professional relationships that enable nurses to carry out necessary teaching and counseling activities. In other settings, the length of stay is so short that there is insufficient time for nurses to do more than maintain the inmate's general health through screening and emergency interventions.

Nurses practicing in correctional facilities provide health care services as their sole responsibility, and matters of nursing judgment are solely their province. Therefore, it is inappropriate for nurses to be involved in the security aspects of the facility and registered nurses would not participate in procedures performed solely for correctional purposes. It is also inappropriate for nurses to participate in disciplinary decisions or committees or to participate directly or indirectly in executions by lethal injection. However, security regulations applicable to facility personnel also apply to health personnel.

Historical Perspectives and Trends

ANA/American Correctional Health Services Association Organizational Units

ANA councils are organizational units through which individual members of state nurses associations participate in improving or advancing the profession in an area of nursing practice or interest. The councils provide a community of peers and a principal source of expertise in the areas of interest and serve as a forum for discussing relevant issues and concerns. They develop standards, positions, and policies for recommendation to the Congress of Nursing Practice. The councils propose the establishment of certification offerings and recommend specific certification requirements in an area of interest to the appropriate governing structures. Currently, there are six councils, which are as follows:

1. Council for Acute Care Nursing Practice
2. Council for Advanced Practice Nursing
3. Council for Community, Primary, and Long Term Care
4. Council for Nursing Research
5. Council for Nursing Systems and Administration
6. Council for Professional Nursing Education and Development.

The ANA Council on Community, Primary, and Long Term Nursing Practice affiliates includes nurses involved in caring for the community, and for individuals who are well, at risk for health problems, or in need of long term care (e.g., in the home, schools, public health agencies, community health clinics or other community-based agencies, work sites, correctional facilities, ambulatory care clinics, provider offices, or nursing homes).

The American Correctional Health Services Association (ACHSA) is the membership organization for all correctional health care professionals. It serves as a forum for current issues and needs confronting correctional health care. It provides education, skill development, and support for personnel, organizations, and decision makers involved in correctional health services, thus contributing to a sense of community and creating positive health changes for detained and incarcerated individuals. The *Scope and Standards of Nursing Practice in Correctional Facilities* published by the American Nurses Association is adopted as ACHSA policy.

Changes in Population and Services

Over 1.3 million persons are incarcerated in the United States, and approximately 1 in every 428 adult residents was in jail on June 30, 1992.[9] According to Bureau of Justice Statistics, the inmate population has doubled over the past decade and is currently growing at the rate of 14 percent yearly. During the same 10 years, the number of incarcerated women tripled in state and federal prisons and doubled in jails.[10,11]

Overall, inmates are poor and undereducated, and ethnic minority populations are disproportionately represented.[12,13] Before incarceration the inmate's lower socioeconomic status tends to limit access to health care services, thereby contributing to higher than average risk for heart disease, hypertension, diabetes, and other chronic illnesses, such as hepatitis, addictive disorders, and mental illness. Because of a significant history of substance abuse, inmates have rates of infection for human immunodeficiency virus (HIV), tuberculosis, hepatitis B, and sexually transmitted diseases that far exceed those of other populations.[14]

Beliefs

The basic philosophy underlying these standards is that health care provided in the correctional facility should be equivalent to that available in the community and subject to the same regulations. The Supreme Court of the United States recognizes that detainees in correctional facilities are totally dependent on the employees of the institution for their health care. This increases the nurse's responsibility for assisting the incarcerated persons with their health care problems.

Ensuring inmates' human rights is of major importance in the controlled environment of correctional facilities. Justice, a cardinal concept guiding the nursing profession, mandates that all persons receive nursing services that are equitable in terms of accessibility, availability, and quality.

Nursing shares in the belief that learning is a lifelong process and demonstrates such through certification of continued education and competency.

Nursing Practice in Correctional Facilities

The major thrust of nursing care in correctional settings is the provision of primary care services for the population. Primary health services in this field include screening activities, providing direct health care services, analyzing individual health behaviors, teaching, counseling, and assisting individuals in assuming responsibility for their own health to the best of their ability, knowledge, and circumstances.

Basic Nursing Practice

Nursing care may be provided in collaboration with other nurses or health professionals, or independently, which is often the case in a small or rural facility. The practice includes providing a full range of nursing services emphasizing disease prevention and health promotion activities, recognizing and treating illnesses and injuries, counseling, and evaluating the effectiveness of planned care.

Advanced Nursing Practice

Advanced nursing practice in correctional facilities is characterized by depth and breadth of knowledge in a nursing specialty and the ability to incorporate knowledge of the correctional field in planning, implementing, and managing health care. The advanced practice nurse guides the practice and critical thinking of nursing and other health care personnel; carries out direct advanced clinical practice; manages one or more clinical practice settings; incorporates scientific knowledge from other disciplines into practice and management; and evaluates the health care provided in those settings.

STANDARDS OF CARE

Standard I. Assessment

The nurse collects client health data.

Rationale

Correctional nursing practice is characterized by a high degree of autonomy and requires a broad-base collection of subjective and objective data.

Measurement Criteria

1. The priority of data collection is determined by the client's immediate condition or needs.
2. Pertinent data are collected by using appropriate assessment techniques, adapted to ensure security and provider safety.
3. Data collection involves the client, significant others, health care providers, and other criminal justice system personnel, when appropriate.
4. The data collection process is systematic and ongoing.
5. Relevant data are documented in a retrievable form.

Standard II. Diagnosis

The nurse analyzes the assessment data in determining diagnoses.

Rationale

The nurse in a correctional facility uses independent judgment and available data to formulate diagnoses.

Measurement Criteria

1. Diagnoses are derived from assessment data.

2. Diagnoses are validated with the client, significant others, health care providers, and records maintained by other institutions, when possible.

3. Diagnoses are documented in a manner that facilitates the determination of expected outcomes and care plan.

Standard III. Outcome Identification

The nurse identifies expected outcomes individualized to the client.

Rationale

The nurse in the correctional facility identifies outcomes based on unique factors (such as length of stay, overall safety, and a lack of information about the prior health status of clients) that affect the nurse's ability to provide services.

Measurement Criteria

1. Outcomes are derived from the diagnoses.

2. Outcomes are documented as measurable goals.

3. Outcomes are mutually formulated with the client and health care providers, when possible.

4. Outcomes are realistic in relation to the client's present and potential capabilities.

5. Outcomes are attainable in relation to resources available to the client.

6. Outcomes include a time estimate for attainment.

7. Outcomes provide direction for continuity of care.

Standard IV. Planning

The nurse develops a care plan that prescribes interventions to attain expected outcomes.

Rationale

Effective planning is essential for appropriate interventions.

Measurement Criteria

1. The plan is individualized to the client's condition or needs.
2. The plan is developed with the client, significant others, health care providers, and other criminal justice system personnel, when appropriate.
3. The plan reflects current nursing practice.
4. The plan is documented.
5. The plan provides for continuity of care from the time of entry into the system, through transfers to other institutions, to final release from custody, when appropriate.
6. The plan provides for discharge follow-up based on the client's need for health care, when appropriate.

Standard V. Implementation

The nurse implements the interventions identified in the care plan.

Rationale

The nurse is the most appropriate health care provider in the correctional setting for ensuring that actions are taken to meet the physical, mental, and health education needs of the client.

Measurement Criteria

1. Interventions are consistent with the established care plan.
2. Interventions are implemented in a safe, appropriate, and timely manner.
3. Interventions are documented.

Standard VI. Evaluation

The nurse evaluates the client's progress toward attainment of outcomes.

Rationale

The nurse in the correctional setting uses the nursing process to evaluate the outcome of nursing actions, interventions, and client education. The nurse may alter the care plan, expand the database, introduce new interventions, and develop client education activities.

Measurement Criteria

1. Evaluation is systematic and ongoing.
2. The client's responses to interventions are documented.
3. The effectiveness of interventions is evaluated in relation to outcomes.
4. Ongoing assessment data are used to revise diagnoses, outcomes, and the care plan, as needed.
5. Revisions in diagnoses, outcomes, and the care plan are documented.
6. The client, significant others, health care providers, and other criminal justice system personnel are involved in the evaluation process, when appropriate.

STANDARDS OF PROFESSIONAL PERFORMANCE

Standard I. Quality of Care

The nurse systematically evaluates the quality and effectiveness of nursing practice.

Rationale

The nurse in the correctional setting ensures that quality nursing care meets measurable community standards.

Measurement Criteria

1. The nurse participates in quality-of-care activities as appropriate to the individual's position, education, and practice environment. Such activities may include the following:
   a. Identifying aspects of care important for quality monitoring.
   b. Identifying indicators used to monitor the quality and effectiveness of nursing care.
   c. Collecting data to monitor the quality and effectiveness of nursing care.
   d. Analyzing quality data to identify opportunities for improving care.
   e. Formulating recommendations to improve nursing practice or client outcomes.
   f. Implementing activities to enhance the quality of nursing practice.
   g. Participating in the work of interdisciplinary teams that evaluate clinical practice or health services.
   h. Developing policies and procedures to improve the quality of care.
2. The nurse uses the results of quality-of-care activities to initiate changes in practice.

3. The nurse uses the results of quality-of-care activities to initiate changes throughout the health care delivery system, as appropriate.

Standard II. Performance Appraisal

The nurse evaluates his/her own nursing practice in relation to professional practice standards and relevant statutes and regulations.

Rationale

The nurse in the correctional setting balances professional performance with the maintenance of safety and security.

Measurement Criteria

1. The nurse regularly engages in performance appraisal, identifying areas of strength as well as areas for professional and practice development.
2. The nurse seeks constructive feedback regarding his/her own practice.
3. The nurse takes action to achieve goals identified during performance appraisal.
4. The nurse participates in peer review as appropriate.

Standard III. Education

The nurse acquires and maintains current knowledge in nursing practice.

Rationale

The diverse health care needs in the correctional facility and the attendant need for nursing autonomy require the nurse to engage in ongoing education.

Measurement Criteria

1. The nurse participates in ongoing educational activities related to clinical knowledge and professional issues.
2. The nurse seeks experiences to maintain clinical skills.

3. The nurse seeks knowledge and skills appropriate to the practice setting.

Standard IV. Collegiality

The nurse contributes to the professional development of peers, colleagues, and others.

Rationale

The nurse in the correctional facility has the responsibility and opportunity to positively influence peers, colleagues, and others regarding health care issues, education, and practice.

Measurement Criteria

1. The nurse shares knowledge, skills, and information with peers, colleagues (including other criminal justice system personnel), and others.
2. The nurse provides peers with constructive feedback regarding their practice.
3. The nurse contributes to an environment that is conducive to the clinical education of nursing students, as appropriate.

Standard V. Ethics

The nurse's decisions and actions on behalf of clients are determined in an ethical manner.

Rationale

The nurse in the correctional setting has an ethical commitment to the client and the nursing profession that must not be compromised.

Measurement Criteria

1. The nurse's practice is guided by the *Code for Nurses*[15] and related ANA position statements, such as the *Position Statement on Nurses' Participation in Capital Punishment*.[16]
2. The nurse maintains client confidentiality.
3. The nurse acts as a client advocate.

4. The nurse delivers care in a nonjudgmental and nondis-criminatory manner that is sensitive to client diversity.

5. The nurse delivers care in a manner that preserves and protects client autonomy, dignity, and rights.

6. The nurse seeks available resources to help formulate ethical decisions.

Standard VI. Collaboration

The nurse collaborates with the client, significant others, other criminal justice system personnel, and health care providers in providing client care.

Rationale

The nurse in the correctional facility collaborates with public and private health care providers to ensure comprehensive continuity of services.

Measurement Criteria

1. The nurse communicates with the client, significant others, criminal justice system personnel, and health care providers regarding client care and nursing's role in the provision of such care.

2. The nurse consults with health care providers for client care, as needed.

3. The nurse makes referrals, including provisions for continuity of care, as needed.

Standard VII. Research

The nurse uses research findings in practice.

Rationale

Utilization and practice of research activities within the correctional setting promotes the professional development and knowledge base within this unique setting. The nurse is expected to adhere to research method guidelines.

Measurement Criteria

1. The nurse uses interventions substantiated by research as appropriate to the individual's position, education, and practice environment.

2. The nurse participates in research activities as appropriate to the individual's position, education, and practice environment. Such activities may include the following:
   a. Identifying clinical problems suitable for nursing research.
   b. Participating in data collection.
   c. Participating in a unit, organization, or community research committee or program.
   d. Sharing research activities with others.
   e. Conducting research within the guidelines of the individual facility, statutes, and regulations.
   f. Critiquing research for application to practice.
   g. Using research findings in the development of policies, procedures, and guidelines for client care.

Standard VIII. Resource Utilization

The nurse considers factors related to safety, effectiveness, and cost in planning and delivering client care.

Rationale

The nurse in the correctional facility is uniquely positioned to determine the priority, availability, and appropriateness of resources required to meet the client's health care needs.

Measurement Criteria

1. The nurse evaluates factors related to safety, effectiveness, efficiency, and cost when two or more practice options would result in the same expected client outcome.

2. The nurse assigns tasks or delegates care based on the needs of the client and on the knowledge and skill of the provider selected.

3. The nurse assists the client and significant others in identifying and securing appropriate, available services to address health-related needs.

REFERENCES

1. American Nurses Association. 1991. *Standards of Clinical Nursing Practice*. Washington, DC: American Nurses Publishing.

2. American Nurses Association. 1993 (February). *Nursing's Agenda for Health Care Reform*. Washington, DC: American Nurses Publishing.

3. American Nurses Association. 1991. *Standards of Clinical Nursing Practice*. Washington, DC: American Nurses Publishing.

4. American Nurses Association. 1988. *Rehabilitation Nursing: Scope of Practice; Process and Outcome Criteria for Selected Diagnoses*. Washington, DC: American Nurses Publishing.

5. American Nurses Association. 1987. *The Scope of Nursing Practice*. Washington, DC: American Nurses Publishing.

6. American Nurses Association. 1985. *Code for Nurses with Interpretive Statements*. Washington, DC: American Nurses Publishing.

7. American Nurses Association. 1980. *Nursing: A Social Policy Statement*. Washington, DC: American Nurses Publishing.

8. American Nurses Association. 1980. *Nursing: A Social Policy Statement*. Kansas City, MO: The Author. pp. 19–29.

9. Bureau of Justice Statistics. 1993 (August). *Correctional Populations in the United States, 1991* (Document No. NCJ-142729). Washington, DC: U.S. Department of Justice.

10. Bureau of Justice Statistics. 1991. *Women in Prison* (Document No. NCJ-1279991). Washington, DC: U.S. Department of Justice.

11. Bureau of Justice Statistics. 1993. *Jail Inmates 1992* (Document No. NCJ-143284). Washington, DC: U.S. Department of Justice.

12. Bureau of Justice Statistics. 1993. *Jail Inmates 1992* (Document No. NCJ-143284). Washington, DC: U.S. Department of Justice.

13. Bureau of Justice Statistics. 1991 (April). *Profile of Jail Inmates, 1989* (Document No. NCJ-129097). U.S. Department of Justice.

14. Glaser, J.B., and Griefinger, R.B. 1993. Correctional health care: A public health opportunity. *Annals of Internal Medicine* 118; 139–145.

15. American Nurses Association. 1985. *Code for Nurses with Interpretive Statements.* Washington, DC: American Nurses Publishing.

16. American Nurses Association. 1988. *Position Statement on Nurses' Participation in Capital Punishment.* Washington, DC: The Author.

INDEX

Pages in the 1995 *Scope and Standards of Nursing Practice in Correctional Facilities* are marked by the year in brackets [1995].

A

Academy of Correctional Health
    Professionals, 6
Administration, 5, 7, 12–13, 14, 16
  ethics and, 41
  leadership and, 46
  professional practice evaluation and,
    36
Advanced practice corrections nursing,
    9, 10, 12
  [1995] 61–62, 66
  assessment, 19
  collaboration, 38
  collegiality, 37
  consultation, 28
  coordination of care, 25
  diagnosis, 20
  education, 35
  ethics, 40
  evaluation, 30
  health teaching and health
    promotion, 26
  implementation, 24
  leadership, 46–47
  outcomes identification, 21
  planning, 22–23
  prescriptive authority and treatment,
    29
  professional practice evaluation, 36
  quality of practice, 33–34
  research, 42
  resource utilization, 44
  See also Corrections nursing; Generalist
    practice corrections nursing
Advanced Practice Registered Nurse
    (APRN), 10
Advocacy, 6, 8, 14, 15, 17
  ethics and, 40
  [1995] 73
  in generalist practice, 10, 12

Age-appropriate care, 3, 15–16
  planning and, 22
  professional practice evaluation and,
    36
  See also Cultural competence
Alternative healthcare models, 17
American Correctional Association
    (ACA), 6, 11, 13, 14
American Correctional Health Services
    Association (ACHSA), 6
  [1995] 64
American Nurses Association (ANA), *vii*, 6
  [1995] 61, 64
  *Code of Ethics for Nurses with
    Interpretive Statements*, *vii*, 14, 40
  Congress on Nursing Practice, *vii*
  [1995] 64
  *Nursing: Scope and Standards of
    Practice*, *vii*
  Nursing's Social Policy Statement, *vii*
  [1995] 61
  *Position Statement on Nurses'
    Participation in Capital Punishment*,
    [1995] 73
American Nurses Credentialing Center
    (ANCC), 14
American Public Health Association
    (APHA), 11
Analysis. *See* Critical thinking, analysis,
    and synthesis
Assessment, 10, 11
  [1995] 61
  defined, 49
  diagnosis and, 20
  [1995] 67
  evaluation and, 30
  [1995] 70
  planning and, 23
  standard of practice, 19
  [1995] 67

79

Criteria (*continued*)
  implementation, 24
    [1995] 69
  leadership, 46–47
  outcomes identification, 21
    [1995] 68
  planning, 22–23
    [1995] 68–69
  prescriptive authority and treatment,
    29
  professional practice evaluation, 36
    [1995] 72
  quality of practice, 33–34
    [1995] 71–72
  research, 42–43
    [1995] 74–75
  resource utilization, 44–45
    [1995] 75–76
Critical thinking, analysis, and synthesis,
    10, 17
  [1995] 66
  assessment and, 19
  consultation and, 28
  coordination of care and, 25
  diagnosis and, 20
    [1995] 67
  evaluation and, 30, 31
  health teaching and health promotion,
    26
  leadership and, 46
  quality of practice and, 33, 34
    [1995] 71
  research and, 42, 43
    [1995] 75
  resource utilization and, 44
Cultural competence, 7
  ethics and, [1995] 74
  health teaching and health promotion,
    26
  outcomes identification and, 21
  planning and, 22, 23
  professional practice evaluation and,
    36
  See also Age-appropriate care

D
Data (defined), 49

Data collection
  assessment and, 19
    [1995] 67
  quality of practice and, 33
    [1995] 71
  research and, 42
    [1995] 75
Decision-making, 10, 12
  [1995] 64
  collaboration and, 38
  consultation and, 28
  coordination of care and, 25
  ethics and, 41
  leadership and, 47
  planning and, 23
  professional practice evaluation and,
    36
  research and, 42
Diagnosis, 10
  defined, 49–50
  evaluation and, 30
    [1995] 70
  outcomes identification and, [1995]
    68
  planning and, 22, 23
  prescriptive authority and treatment,
    29
  standard of practice, 20
    [1995] 67–68
Disease (defined), 50
Documentation, 11, 16
  assessment and, 19
    [1995] 67
  collaboration and, 38, 39
  coordination of care and, 25
  diagnosis and, 20
    [1995] 68
  education and, 35
  evaluation and, 30, 31
    [1995] 70
  implementation and, 24
    [1995] 69
  outcomes identification and, 21
    [1995] 68
  planning and, 22
    [1995] 69
  quality of practice and, 33

E

Economic issues. *See* Cost control

Eddy, Thomas, 5

Education of corrections nurses, 7, 10–11, 12–13, 16
  [1995] 62, 64, 66
  collaboration and, 38
  collegiality and, 37
    [1995] 73
  quality of practice and, [1995] 71
  research and, [1995] 75
  standard of professional performance, 35
    [1995] 72–73
  See also Mentoring; Professional development

Education of patients and families, 7, 8, 9, 10, 15
  [1995] 63, 66
  evaluation and, [1995] 70
  prescriptive authority and treatment, 29
  resource utilization and, 44
  See also Family; Health teaching and health promotion; Patient

Environment (defined), 50
  See also Practice environment

Estelle v. Gamble, 1–2
  See also Laws, statutes, and regulations

Ethics, 7, 11, 12, 14–15
  outcomes identification and, 21
  quality of practice and, 33
  standard of professional performance, 40–41
    [1995] 73–74
  See also Code of Ethics for Nurses with Interpretive Statements; Laws, statutes, and regulations

Evaluation, 9, 10, 12
  [1995] 61, 62, 66
  defined, 50
  health teaching and health promotion, 26
  leadership and, 46
  resource utilization and, 44, 45
  standard of practice, 30–31
    [1995] 70

Evidence-based practice
  assessment and, 19
  consultation and, 28
  defined, 50
  education and, 35
  implementation and, 24
  leadership and, 47
  outcomes identification and, 21
  planning and, 23
  prescriptive authority and treatment, 29
  quality of practice and, 34
  See also Research

Expected outcomes (defined), 50

F

Family, 7
  [1995] 61, 62
  assessment and, 19
    [1995] 67
  collaboration and, 38
    [1995] 74
  defined, 50
  diagnosis and, 20
    [1995] 68
  evaluation and, 30, 31
    [1995] 70
  health teaching and health promotion, 26
  outcomes identification and, 21
  planning and, 22
    [1995] 69
  resource utilization and, 44
    [1995] 76
  See also Education of patients and families; Patient

Financial issues. *See* Cost control

G

Generalist practice corrections nursing, 10–12
  [1995] 61–62, 66
  assessment, 19
    [1995] 67
  collaboration, 38
    [1995] 74
  collegiality, 37
    [1995] 73

Outcomes (*continued*)
  diagnosis and, 20
    [1995] 68
  ethics and, 40, 41
  evaluation and, 30
    [1995] 70
  implementation and, 24
  leadership and, 47
  planning and, 22
    [1995] 68
  quality of practice and, 33
    [1995] 71
  resource utilization and, 44, 45
    [1995] 75
  See also Outcomes identification
Outcomes identification
  standard of practice, 21
    [1995] 68
  See also Outcomes

P
Parents. *See* Family
Patient, 7
  [1995] 61, 62, 63
  assessment and, 19
    [1995] 67
  collaboration and, 38
    [1995] 74
  consultation and, 28
  defined, 51
  diagnosis and, 20
    [1995] 68
  ethics and, 40
  evaluation and, 30, 31
    [1995] 70
  health teaching and health
    promotion, 26
  outcomes identification and, 21
    [1995] 68
  planning and, 22
    [1995] 69
  prescriptive authority and treatment,
    29
  professional practice evaluation and,
    36
  resource utilization and, 44
    [1995] 75, 76

See also Education of patients and
    families; Family
Peer review, [1995] 61
  collegiality and, 37
    [1995] 73
  defined, 51
  professional practice evaluation and,
    36
    [1995] 72
Pill line, 11
Planning, 10, 12, 14
  [1995] 61, 62, 63, 66
  collaboration and, 38, 39
  consultation and, 28
  coordination of care and, 25
  defined, 51
  diagnosis and, 20
    [1995] 68
  evaluation and, 30
    [1995] 70
  implementation and, 24
  outcomes identification and, 21
    [1995] 68
  resource utilization and, 44, 45
  standard of practice, 22–23
    [1995] 68–69
Policy. *See* Healthcare policy
Population served, 2–4, 5, 8, 9
  [1995] 63, 65
Practice environment, 1–2, 5–6, 7, 9, 10
  [1995] 63
  collegiality and, 37
    [1995] 73
  education and, 35
    [1995] 73
  leadership and, 46
  in measurement criteria, 19, 21, 25, 26,
    34, 36, 37, 40, 42, 44, 46
  quality of practice and, [1995] 71
  research and, [1995] 75
Practice roles. *See* Roles in corrections
    nursing practice
Practice settings. *See* Practice
    environment
Preceptors. *See* Mentoring
Prescriptive authority and treatment, 12
  standard of practice, 29

Index   **87**